# Secrets That Speak

ALANA EDA JOHNSON

# Author's Note

I began writing the majority of this collection of poetry when I was still in high school, which is why it exudes a younger feel. The second half onward was written more recently, making this collection a time capsule of my experiences, worries, insecurities, losses and lessons. While compiling this collection, I was startled to find I no longer held the same resentment, bitterness or despondence I'd felt during the time of writing each poem. Instead, I tended to look back on these experiences with a new fondness and nostalgia. I found comedic relief in the things I used to antagonize over, liberation in the things I believed bound me.

That is not to say, I don't *still* relate to many of the themes I wrote about. I still have trouble making friends, trusting in myself and letting go of the things that don't benefit me, but as I look at all that I've gained in spite of the losses, I don't lose any more sleep over it.

Writing and publishing my own words has always been a dream of mine, however now that the moment is upon me, it is as terrifying as it is exhilarating. I've been working on a series of novels since I was a little girl, but those words told other people's stories. These words are all me. All about my own life, my own faults, my own flaws, shortcomings and weaknesses. I cannot shield myself behind a fictional character and I believe that makes poetry all the more magical.

In this book, I hope you all feel welcome and find one or two poems to relate to. To my young girls and young women readers especially, this is all for you; everything I do, is for you- for *us*. And to my Turkish readers: bana her zaman ait olduğumu hissettiren Türk okuyucularıma, Türk halkıma teşekkür etmek istiyorum.

If you've picked up this book, I want to thank every single one of you for supporting my dream, for caring about what I have to say and especially for hearing me.

Love,
Alana Eda Johnson ♡

# CONTENTS

# youth

# The 2000's

Growing up in the 2000's made everything feel brand new. Every stone unturned, everything made to *seem* perfectly neat and tidy to hide the messy. We weren't yet politically correct or technologically savvy, appearances were all we had, see-

We'd only just begun learning to wield words on our tongues, then make them legible- *intelligible* on a page. Blinked to find mathematics makes the world run. It's also something I've never quite gotten the hang of. And in between learning diluted, *deluded* versions of history and the proper technique to kick a ball around the schoolyard, we learned to play the recorder, to obey orders, to do group projects; teamwork.

Back then, trees felt short enough to reach and the tallest thing *in reach*, so we climbed them. Chased each other till we were winded. Made our own fun and games- till the computers came; a thing to be obeyed had captured our fascination plain as day, said: *we can give you... **everything.***

I remember sleeping and waking, the next morning, the chalkboard was smart, slick, quick. They called it: the SMARTboard. Said it was a step towards the future. An uninvited but welcome guest, this new invention no one was keen on escorting off the premises. Our teachers insisted we get used to having the SMARTboard around, though I don't remember the discussion that prompted this. Don't remember being asked if we *wanted* to get used to it, if we missed yesterday, if we missed the old way of doing things.

I *do* remember when the unsolved equations kept involuntarily erasing. I'd started thinking maybe this *could* be a good thing:

because the clock kept ticking and our algebra teacher was running out of ways to convince us to find Y and "Fix the goddamn SMARTboard" at the same time.

I remember sleeping and waking. The next morning, I'd stopped dwelling on the old way. Instead began considering why we'd ever thought it to be plausible in the first place. Why did we ever think it to be anything other than primitive? Why hadn't we been granted this gift to begin with? How had we been robbed, been *deceived* like this? Once upon a time, the chalk had squealed like a dying rodent caught between my prepubescent fist, drawing attention to my own apprehension. I remember sleeping and waking, the next morning, the SMARTboard was fixed; had acclimated to our inferiority, our indolence.

Now with the changeling chalk in my fist, unaware of the answer to Y, I had to consider: was I... *lagging?*

Nostalgia's been a word I've hated with a passion. Guess I've always wanted to look back on my youth with a detached sort of fondness, because I was so far past it. Yet the aftertaste is lingering and bitter, always after a chase: a resentful wraith.

I can't help but marvel at growing up in the 2000's, a new dawn, a new world post 9/11. Everyone says today is scary for children to play in. So I suppose I *am* nostalgic, suppose I *am* swarmed and surrounded by its after effects.

Pulling the trigger meant our opponents were soaked wet. Career Day had us wanting to be aerospace engineers. During lunch period, we constructed paper airplanes with a concentration so severe, you'd think we intended to fly them, carry passengers and cargo. We were so *guileless*, our innocence was limited, but I remember the way we thought we'd be living; answering standardized test questions about flying automobiles and dinosaurs reincarnated, roaming the Earth among us.

I've always wanted a big life, with the right words to articulate each and every experience. As if a life you could *retell* would warrant a cover and a spine. As if that sort of life would make up for all the things I consider lacking, consider missing links. Now I'm beginning to think that all this time... maybe we shouldn't have been in such a big hurry.

Gifted, golden, promising young women wanted the hips, prefrontal cortex, the autonomy. Wanted friends and new hobbies, wanted the glory, I wanted to be somebody. And now I think I'll always be seven, twelve, fifteen, thinking... is this all meant to mean something?

Remember playing hide-n-seek with my cousin in the apartment we grew up in. After years of the game, we raised the stakes and the objective became less about seeking, less about being *found*, but rather about just how clever you could *seem*, just how quiet you could be. How strategically you could bend and mold your body, pushing it well past its limits, just to make it fit, just to camouflage; just to fit **in.**

Then we grew up. Now well-versed in hiding in plain sight. Seated in a crowded room, so well hidden... they never found me again.

I wish I was excited for every Christmas again. I wish wearing high heels was worth all the anticipation. I wish rereading the last page held the same weight. Wish someone had said: find delight in the season's first snow. Watch reruns of 90's sitcoms- pretend not to know. It's your last round of musical chairs, of hopscotch, of Double Dutch. Lucky Charms *will* make that cereal, strictly marshmallows: they heard us. One last tea party. It's a Monday and not Halloween morning, but I want to wear my fairy wings to get groceries. My mood ring said it'd please me. One last *Nancy Drew* mystery.

It seems, we were the last children to indulge in ignorance- in innocence. And by God, wasn't it bliss? I wish someone had told us, it won't always be like this, but you will always crave it, strain to reach that unscratchable itch.

You *will* want the 2000's back, I promise.

# Child's Play

The boys *feel* their jeans
writhing at their ankles.
Chain belts thick gunmetal.
Cackling hysterical.

They'd committed crimes.
And children don't know tired
when it's a game and the game is chase.
Schoolyard an urban underbelly,
cops at their heels.

I suppose this had been a sort of conditioning.

When the boys got this *glint* in their eye
more fierce than the sun; arguing
over which game was worth their while,
let's have a moment of silence
for the universe's equilibrium,
for ramifications.

Our boys *were* cops.
Desperate to prove they were no imitation.
Yanking robber's wrists taut behind their backs.
Limp in handcuffs, grip inelastic as their grins.

Our boys grew up.
Now when they flee on foot,
it's a manhunt. Once the best game.

It'd arrest our breaths, heartbeat
pounding in our ears something terrific.

It was fun then,
when everyone cooperated.
When we were all just playing.
When it was just a game.

Urban underbelly.
Cops catch up.
It's a boot in the neck,
between the shoulderblades.
Handcuffs so tight, heartbeat untamed.
"I can't **breathe**!"

Supposed to say ten days.
Now it's a ten year sentence
for a crime our boys didn't commit.
One day before recess, we'd learned
about the Sixth Amendment.
A spectacled boy suggested a trial
during a water break. Our boys smacked
him upside the head, sniggering.

Our teachers encouraged us
to use big words with more substance
than good or bad. But on Career Day,
cops were as simple as that:

Good People catching Bad People.
Good People doing the Good Thing.
And we wanted to be Good People
doing Good Things, so we looked up
to the real things.

Now our boys look up
at the policemen from the ground,
feeling juvenile for expecting them
to be Good People doing the Good Thing.
Our boys wonder if their grown-upness
now made *them* the best game: Fugitive.

A boy was tagged once.
They dug their hands in his fro
when they ought to yank him
by the wrists. Tugged so hard
he fell, split open his lip.

He just laughed,
said he wasn't the fugitive
they were looking for.
The real perp was behind the fence,
getting away with it. None of our boys
were in the *mood* to believe him.

Because wasn't it way more fun to be arrested?
And didn't prison just suit him?

# How The Film Ends

The first snow's become slush; knee-deep and revolting,
but the Christmas lights go up early. Glittering bright
and identical as every Christmas before this one.

Everyone gathers round the bodega cashier.
Having braved the weather for lone roles
of off-brand toilet paper, Scratch-Offs,
hot chips and mild conversation.
Ask how his daughter's been.
He gives me the second bag free.

This misplaced happiness, I still search for it.
That inexplicable contentment.
Chinese takeout menu taped to the fridge.
Scan it as though we plan to go off script.
Restaurant owner throws in an extra Sprite
free of charge, rattles off our orders by heart.

Humming radiator.
Yappy Jack Russell Terrier.
No cable so it's roulette.
What'll we land on today?
Conversation so good,
laugh till we're crying.

If I manage to stay very still,
I can feel our ghosts
sidled alongside me now;

unaware of the imminent eviction,
notice signed *Circumstance.*
It wasn't perfect.
It wasn't planned.
Should've known how the film ends.

# Chocolate Cake

Eyes skim disinterested over passerby
and life transpiring, instead of at each other.
It's been *like* a long time.

This occasion is commemorated
with garden salad and stale fries
and idle commentary on others' lives,
because we've nothing to talk about.
Offhand laughter out of tune.
No more echoed see you soon's.

No room to seek her hand across the table.
Though it is empty and I am able.
Rather I marvel at new age spots,
acquainted with each annual follow up.

It's been *like* a long time.
This occasion is commemorated
with chocolate cake. She demands it
be our picture perfect centerpiece.
Never mind, I hate chocolate
so it will go uneaten.

Chocolate cake drenched in such syrup, I'm beguiled.
And just to *be* something- she feigns surprise.
Chocolate cake an insinuation of old times.
Wouldn't leave her lap then. Now I'm exhausted.
Besides, I was never any good at playing pretend.

The unfinished chocolate cake is taken away.
She doesn't protest, which is unusual
for someone ordinarily stingy with
their money. Today she's at ease.

Just fastens her coat, looks onward.
Pleased it's all over with, because she
was getting bored of it. Says she's sated.
Says it was more than enough to remind
her of what sugar tastes like, after so long.

Mere moments past noon.
She says it's getting dark.
She says we've sat long enough.
She says "Alright, that's enough."
**I've** had more than enough

# Uncondensed

Am I a fool to want to know everything?

The milk's expired. Left in the fridge
by your forgetful father. Catalyst for the
detour, getting coffee at the new shop
cross the block, rather than down the street,
where your 8:30 bus will meet.

All this, because your usual coffee shop was closed
for repairs, brought on by the mini kitchen fire,
immediately extinguished by frantic new employees
before the manager arrived punctually at 9:15.

Am I wrong- flawed in my dissatisfaction with:
"I was almost late to work grabbing coffee"?

# Defective

I am tired of being second best. Succumbing to it
because it seeks in me, camaraderie. Rotate behind
the others voluntarily, when the sidewalk's narrowing.
Because afterthoughts don't hesitate.

My so-called friends *do* remember to look back
for me, when we reach the station. What would've
happened, if I hadn't been taking the same train?

Is something the matter with me?
Perhaps I was born with some ghastly deficiency.
Not exactly mesmerizing, but some kind of alright,
till the second hour of our honeyed time together.

"So there is a next time… right?"
Stale laughter answers my accidental insinuation.
They never intended to see me… again.

Is this my curse to bear, being regarded only
by the absent mind? Liability. Only slightly lovely,
when it is I, utterly devoted till the end of time.

Am I the meekest lion to have ever lived?
Unable to discard the remains.
Pocketing souvenirs of the chase.

I let them go their own way.
Can't exactly say please stay.
Haughty set of my chin is fake
as the fruitless concept of friendship.

Rip off the bandaid in the dark
and only then, do I cry out.
It's not as if they can hear me now.

# girlhood

# April

If April were a girl,
they'd call her *just* pretty, I can tell.
She'd wear ribbons in her hair
and crepe pleated skirts that cutoff
at her knees, ruffling in her own spring
breeze. And she'd smell like tulips.
Never perfume, strictly body mist.

We all wanted to be April at one time or another.
Wanted to be April's bruised knees
when she tripped for the first time.
Merely bruised, never bloody.

We all wanted to be April at one time or another.
Just like our mothers and their mothers.
They'd never succeeded in resembling her either.
So they named their daughters May, June,
even September, feeling some kind of clever.

Cuts ache though I still yearn
to hold the roses by their thorns.
We're women; incapable of being squeamish
at the sight of a little blood. And besides,
what's a little more in the grand scheme
of *precariously* pretty things?

Because isn't that the marketing?
Isn't it engraved right into the packaging?
Women merely have tasks because *we* are
the objectives they meet. Commodities
not to be wasted- used up till we strain
to recreate the same music; perform
in perfect harmony. And amidst our
discord, April is a perfect symphony.

Yulissa writes the best essays
in class. They still flick up her skirt
to get a glimpse of her ass.
I compliment Jennifer's braids
that are always immaculate.
Her smile arrives so belated,
she looks near mean. Almost-delight's
caught her tight between its teeth.
She still waits for the punchline
even after I've walked away.

Aprils, noncommittal and misfortuned
kiss November's on the lips in hopes
our November skies rub off on them.

Because we get a B minus.
Get our shot in the school play.
Give ourselves bad haircuts.
Play the ukulele. Fingerpaint…
and still wanna be April;
sweet-as-spring, amicable and
of course, pretty. Perfectly unbiased
is her breeze.

Blow out our birthday candles
in hopes of what? Don't exactly know.
Knew we hated her though, or did at least
once or twice. Hated her 'cause she enticed.
Until hating her became a vice.
Hated her because they told us to, told us:
"She's much too pretty to actually be nice."

But they were wrong. She was alright.
Till they primetime paraded her round
the marketplace. Mere bartering piece.
They auction her worth away. They told her:
*You're so pretty, who cares if you even think.*

# Secrets That Speak

They think we're friends.
This isn't an unusual assumption.
If on the off chance you caught
either of us alone and we didn't know
you well enough to have our guard up,
we might agree. We *were* friends.

After all, we sat together all the time
to complain and cram for next period's exam.
Congregated in the cafeteria, guzzling
moody tween girl feelings.

They think we're friends.
This isn't an unusual assumption.
There's strength in numbers for a reason.
Except we had nothing in common
apart from seeking validation, deflecting
middle school gossip and gauging the boys'
new insistence and ever changing demands.

And sure we stepped on each other's toes.
Were cruel, calculated and cold. *But like,
being a girl is like really hard sometimes!*

So we sacrificed true friendship for
outfits in agreement with "the trends".
In harmony with each other's fear
of originality. We shared palates in
music and TV. Affinity for bad mouthing
each other, rarely studying and wearing
boys hoodies like trophies.

Angela was the ringleader. Wasn't decidedly pretty.
Equipped with long, dark hair running straight down
her back. Smart, the best at math and never without
a comeback. Always had name-brand jeans and
a sense of self, whether feigned or genuine?
We could never tell. The upper hand in her step
was apparent and once she caught you, she
never let up- never quit.

Maybe it was seeing her vulnerable for once.
Maybe it was the humiliation; how it reeked.
Reminded us of every weakness we'd been
forced to bury. Now hers lay unguarded,
blatant as the blood under the fluorescent
cafeteria lights.

We were just beginning to get our periods
or had already gotten them. Those ahead
basked in the alleged maturity the rest of us
supposedly lacked.

But now, Angela had bled well past her dark wash
American Eagle jeans. And all of the girls' shrieks
were pitchy, rabid things. Frozen in my seat,
girls parted around me like the Red Sea.

Our eyes were meeting and for once,
Angela's were devoid of any meaning.
Girls scrambling- trampling each other,
just to get away from her. Writhing,
checking their own clothes. And in the
hysteria, one of the girls grabbed my binder.
Some kind of cruel joke.

Justice's sparkly star speckled binder I thought
would make me seem devoted to "the trends",
make me seem more girly back then, had only
invited more catty remarks from them.
And now a girl I'd barely spoken two words to,
waved it like a flag. Giggling manic, threatening
to wipe up Angela's blood with it. Spectacled girl
delighted in my flailing to grab it back.

Angela sat almost in a trance.
Color seeped from her skin.
Frozen, almost certain if she
remained sculpture, no one
would notice her. It was too late.
Our spectacle had garnered attention

from the surrounding tables.
Tactical, practical Angela tried to mop
the blood up with her hands. Tried to
disappear the evidence, while the others
thrived on the payback.

A dean stalked over to establish order and discipline.
Sent Angela running to the nurse. "You're her friends!"
Not an unusual assumption.

"What kind of friends do this?"
This was a shared experience.
A woman thing. We should've
been more understanding.

It was a hybrid of a secret: menstruation.
A tale also known to be true but kept out of view.
Before bedlam ensued there was a moment of
suspended silence. We all stared at the seat, horrified
that the secret now had a mouth of its own...
and could speak.

# Deathbed

The girl in my bed asks:
"What is the worst thing you've ever done,
that you don't regret because it was necessary?"

She is only a bit older than me, lovelier
in her self-assurance. We wear the same
face, so I pine just a little longer.
One day, I'll meet her.

"The truth is…"
I don't have an answer. Pursed lips, blouse riding up
exposing her midriff. She's in the same skin we once
despised. Now, she lounges as if the most magnificent
jungle cat. Unafraid, at home at last.

She tilts her head, with a rueful smile.
"What a shame. I thought you'd have
many wonderful stories to tell me."

The girl in my bed asks:
"What's the funnest, coolest thing
you've ever done, in your whole life?"

She is younger. Still wears her hair in two neat braids.
Gets very angry when kids call them pigtails.
Still wears her hair in two neat braids, because
she despises her hair any and every other way.
Even this one.

For her, I am most sorry I have nothing to tell.
I've kept none of the promises we made
about who we'd be, when we got older.
In her daydreams, we were braver, **bolder.**
Grew up and desired a clean cut life.
Now I play it safer. Color inside the lines
like she once wanted to. She thought it was
the grown up thing to do.

She was always in a hurry to be me
and now I am not who I said I'd be.
Now she looks at me as though
I'd lured her. Always wanted her
to look at me like the end of the
crosswalk she'd dreamed of walking
on her own. When mother would
finally let our hand go.

Now I crumble under her gaze, know she'd be proud.
We read stories of empresses and queens with gazes
so fierce they'd galvanize entire armies, alter histories,
make princes and kings fall to their knees.

She's incredulous. She's ruthless.
"Oh please, you've gotta be kidding me!"

I tell her we sing on great, big stages.
Spit in high school algebra's face.
Made peace with our hair; wear it
uninhibited, the way we will one day
wear our skin. We fell in love and
got over it. We've done so much-
certainly, there's more to say, but when
she looks at me that way...

**What have you done that you can look
back on, besides accomplishments?
What have you done just for the
moment, just for the heck of it?
To laugh at later. Pay reparations
for in the future. Because at least
you can tell your grandchildren-
if you want some, that is.**

Her kid face is puckered.
Calm before the storm.
I don't have the heart to tell her:
You're not me anymore.

# Castaways

The fire went out weeks ago. Your clothes reek,
stiff with sea water. Disillusioned; orbit the isle.
Sun in my eyes, most inhospitable. What a fool
I am for clinging to your hand. The ships have
met shore, restless of waiting for us.

We'd been marooned. Missing. Lonely.
Winter incoming. Ink's all gone.
Can't keep using my blood to write
letters lost to wires crossed.
Fingers behind my back, betting
this time, you'll understand.
While you promenade the island
instead. As if I'll wait forever, Peter.

I'm waxing and waning. The tide comes in.
The seasons'll change. Know you'll leave me
halfway in the last best dress I own.
I do and I don't let go. I get on the ship.
Uncertain, smile lopsided; you don't run
to catch me again. And call me… friend.

Turn back to look ahead.
The captain makes the last call.
I must succumb to be saved.
"Will we be friends forever?"
You nod wordless, try on a smile and wave.

# Little Girl

Night had fallen, but the day was off.
The argument wasn't vicious because I hated
the aftertaste of those kinds. Mother only looking
at me when necessary. More akin to looking
through me. I didn't need it. Didn't need either of our
pettiness, so I'd conceded.

"When you were little, you'd wake and before
breakfast, television or games, I'd hold you
to my chest and we'd read together.
Then we'd begin our day. Do you remember?"

I wanted to call out to my mother.
Suddenly- *irrationally* afraid we'd drifted
too far to reconcile or reach one another.
It was a simpler time.

"Back then we only needed each other."

I've learned to be wary when people
become sentimental. Recounting memories
means they're inquiring about something
and I've never been the intuitive sort.
When my mother tells me how I used to be
closer to her as a little girl, I know she is
asking me to comply- indulge her once more.
I don't know. I've never been the intuitive sort.

# Reflection

Girl in the mirror mere reflection.
Hair's growing back- growing *long*
like mother likes. Want your hair long
this time. Not sixteen anymore; aching
all over for control, within a life you tenant,
that's barely your own. Oftentimes, I speak
without sound. Still live with Mother, just
used to live in a mock-up of a Dream House.

These days, Mother and I have become strangers.
How have you been, on the other side of the kitchen?
These days, refer to them as the old days, the good
days, the golden age.

Having fallen so far, who will stoop to teach
a young woman to walk again? When all I can
do lately is remove my coat. What do *I* want
to be? What will make *you* pleased with me
again, Mommy? Who was she? I'll be her again.

Forgive me.

# Fifteen

Still going through the motions.
Going through some thing- the same things.
Retelling a story, I say "I was fifteen."
Like it's still yesterday. Like I'm not twenty-three.

I was fifteen. I've all the time in the world
to be something- be anything I dream.
I'm fifteen, still living in Queens.
In fact, there's nowhere else I'd rather be.

Christmas time and it isn't just mommy and I.
The house isn't empty. I have so much life to lead.
Just take me back to fifteen.

# Forged Season

In autumn, there is springtime.
Quite surprised, to see our spirits climb
out of the pits of our stomachs and other
secluded places, in which they hide.

Marmalade sunlight falls on her face.
We walk side by side at a similar pace.
Friendship sickly sweet. Gaggle of girls
giggling, depart on diverging streets.
Molten leaves. Sun's warmth hypnotizing.
I drink in the undoubtedly final warm day
we'd received free of charge, the way cactus
take in rain. Promise me we'll always be the same?

The things we don't say, melt into yesterday's
forgotten chill. And I'm smiling so wide,
forgot quite how it felt.

Born under the sun, final week of July.
It's not an understatement: winter makes
me want to die. There's just something
about summer…

Sucked on Blow Pops third period in an almost
drunken haze of lost summer. Can't remember
anybody's name, nor want to when it isn't
summer. What a shame, we're content being
caged, if we're aware at least in some way,
that the outside world we can't see is brighter
and warmer than yesterday.

Tomorrow marks today's funeral.
Wonder what my eulogy will say.
Summer's long gone. So can we at least stay?

# Swan Song

*I can see everything from here!*
See the entire universe and know what
it all means. Three American beauties
tell me why they wished to be queen.
It's only high school, they aren't sure
when they'll get the chance to be so
young and beautiful ever again.

But for the moment, we're all in the choir.
For the moment, we're all friends.
For the moment, everything's hilarious.
No phones allowed, but how else will
we take photographs? Smiling, perspiring,
harmonizing beneath the stage lights.

Sing Bohemian Rhapsody entirely off-key.
Tangible is our vitality. Turn to leave
the last of me you'll ever see.
It's only high school.
We will never reconvene.

For the moment, we're still holding hands.
For the moment, everything's still loud and grand.
For the moment, I won't cry. Had no friends
for four years, have 'em tonight. Who'll hold
open the chasm- keep tonight alive?

Walk me to the station, it'll be alright.
Gotta let go of my hand now. Let go of
everything you thought I'd been.
Draw lines in daylight.
Imposters under the twilight.
Quit asking why I have to go.
It's only high school.
We're already ghosts

# motherland

# Sıkıldım

Last weekend, Mom kept saying she was bored
in Turkish: **sıkıldım.** Kept saying it, like she
was singing a song. A pop song, with too much
background music to make up for the blank
spaces where lyrics should be. **Sıkıldım.**

*My* mother doesn't get like this ever.
*My* mother NEVER lets herself be bored.
*My* mother is always tinkering, reorganizing.
Always tending to something or another.

*My* mother isn't the bored type.
*My* mother will create busy-work.
*My* mother is the queen of productivity.
*My* mother criticizes *me* for sticking
to the couch like I am a part of it.

And last weekend, she was bored.
Bored in Turkish. We are in Turkey.
We live in Turkey... now. Sorry- *Türkiye.*
My mother jabs me in the side with her elbow.
Reminds me never to let them call it Turkey.

Americans were always doing an impression of us.
*Gobble gobble.* I'd fly into a rage when I was a child,
"Stop it, I said stop it right now!"
So it's Türkiye, not Turkey.
"That is not the name of my country!"
Sorry- *our* country.

Last weekend she was bored in Turkish.
I've never heard *my* mother say "I am bored"
in English, ever. I get bored sometimes-
catch it, like sickness or a fever.

But I am peculiar and I don't mean quirky.
I can coax myself out of my own boredom.
An overactive imagination, I think they call it.
All rich Manhattan ladies' sons've got it.
They take pills and talk to people all about it.

My mother is no rich Manhattan lady.
And I'm no rich Manhattan lady's child.
So if my mother's life has become incurably
boring and my maladaptive daydreaming's failing...
Who do we speak to? What even is there to do?

# Cruel Summer

"Summer, I know why you were so cruel."
For the first time in my life, walked instead
of ran into the solace of your arms. Bystander
as winter became spring. Forgot you've no
interest in being appraised. Take fairness by
the lapels, to toss her out into the alleyway
to fend for herself. This time around, you
were red wine and bubblegum coinciding
in my mouth.

Used to cross off the days, finger painting
with my own blood. Now I'm all out of ink.
Meanwhile everyone keeps asking, "Was that
Summer? Where's she going?" As if you
are capable of inornate departure.

I tell you I've had enough over coffee,
most diplomatically. Your laugh humorless
though still honeyed. First sweat above
their brow, they craved you less, begged
for even the slightest breeze. My adoration
for you never waned! You weren't betrayed.
I merely stopped to smell the roses- *admire*
blooming things, before they were long gone.

Forgot you've no interest in being admired
if autumn's *also* fair game. So we part ways
at dawn. I wake to the prelude of autumn's
chill. We'll try again come June. I promise,
this time I'll run to meet you. You can show
me off on a night out on the town.
We'll be better for each other then.
"You're cruel, Summer now."

# Used To

It used to be sunny, always summer, till it wasn't.
Used to rain until some kind of strange drought.
Till all summer into late September, you'd have
to choose between washing your dirty laundry
or your hair. The water'd appear for an hour
at best, then echo through dry pipes, leaving
us to cry out "But it was just there!"

Water slim as a figure on a faulty diet.
Running through our fingers like runoff,
so that all summer into late September,
we'd stink. Used to despise the rain back
in New York. Now I can't imagine a world
without it. Long to hear it's footfalls however
raucous, however loud and obnoxious.
It used to rain a lot the first year I attempted
university in my mother's country. Felt like
such an outsider, it scared me. So I'd stand
in the downpour putting snails back in the earth
safely, so they wouldn't remain underfoot.

The soil used to smell rich and fertile before
the semi-drought. My grandmother used to
cook until she didn't. Used to be happy to
see us, till she wasn't. Everyone used to gather
come summer. Used to call one another.
Now we're all disjointed and bitter. And no one
bothers to call me so I don't call back either.

I used to reek of seawater. Hair bedraggled,
slathered in conditioner in the shower.
Remember the summer I turned twelve.
Frolicked too long, got caught up in the sun.
The kids next year taunted that I was too dark.
Said I looked like an ape. I was too young to know
I'd develop a complex, but next summer, slathered
sunscreen all over my face. What was a white cast?
I was in white-face. My Turkish wasn't fluent but
I understood everyone on the beach laughing,
calling me "yogurt face".

I'm in Istanbul now, tired of questions without
answers. But still can't help but wonder how it
all went wrong so quickly- Bodrum washed
its hands of me. I remember the flight. One way.
Not yet eighteen. Missing home, sick for it.
In sleep, I'd involuntarily scratch at the skin
on my face till it'd bleed. Wake up with
perpendicular gashes thick and mean.

I fell in love with a dream.
With an illusory thing.
Something almost beautiful.
Family photographs. Traditions.
Adap ve usül. Home-cooked meals.

I almost had everything.
I'd almost absconded with something.

# He-Said-She-Said

They say, "Why don't you write something in Turkish,
so we can read it?" I explain that I can always translate
it, when it is published. The same thing I said last year
and the year before that. They just nod, vacant and
unimpressed. Mom says, "Why don't you smile more
Turkish, so that they can feel at ease in its presence?
Your smile is disingenuous. Unfriendly. Too cold.
Your jokes are too American. Turkish people are
hot-blooded. It looks like you're faking it. Smile Eda,
Allah aşkına! You look like you don't want to be here!"

The flight attendants continue to greet Mom in Turkish
and me, attached to her hip like a protruding, faultily
reattached limb, in English. The first time I fly outbound
over the Atlantic alone, I speak to the flight attendants
in my best, most formally dressed Turkish and they smile
so wide, I know I've done it right. My mother is not there
to hear it. And I have half a mind to wonder who I'm
playing dress up- playing pretend for.

My mother calls me a full-blooded American.
She does not yell when she says it, she is matter-of-fact.
I've never felt American. Never felt Turkish entirely.
More an evenly split cookie.

The first time I fly one-way over the Atlantic alone,
after years of saying I'd leave New York behind,
everyone asks me "Hangisi daha iyi?" And I know

my mother is asking it too. In her eyes, there is
umut inşallah, that I would make up my mind.
"Both countries are so different, I couldn't decide."
I say, batting flies. The same thing I said last year
and the year before that. They just nod, vacant
and unimpressed. I want to say, "In America,
we have something called the gray area."
Ama biliyorum Türkler would just call it cowardice.

Not quite Turkish. Not quite American.
Just a New Yorker, wholeheartedly, that's
for sure. New Yorkers romanticize the *notion*
of our mother's home countries, while reciting
The Pledge of Allegiance. Memorizing our
alleged amendments, one of them being free speech.

In Türkiye, you can't say just about anything.
In Türkiye, you can't be a woman and say
just about anything anymore. It is strange,
muzzling myself, I am not unlike my cousin's
yappy Jack Russell Terrier. Perhaps it's why
my mother always tried to teach me it was
better to be a good listener.

I remember being perplexed junior year, by the
lesson on nationalism. I could never understand
peering at something you're stood on and it
appearing from all angles, completely spotless: lekesiz.

# Gnat

She's browsing the aisle with all she's got.
Taking in the space. Taking it *up* willingly.
Dirty blonde and fifteen... probably.

I'm just twenty...lonely.
She's got a friend she doesn't
bother with. They look like twins.
Alleged all-American incarnate.

She's got on flip-flops.
Toenails painted cerulean.
The clothes don't fit her,
she just **fits in** the space she holds.
Baggy hoodie, distressed denim shorts.
Name-brand, I'm sure.

My eyes downcast finally meet hers.
I regret it, my hair a frizzy bedraggled nest.
No match for her face so tightly closed off,
prim and priss. I very much want to sink
into the floor and also want to stay. Not
just in the aisle but in the country; carrying
myself the way she did, walking the way she
walked. Filling the space. Perusing the aisles.
Belonging.

Because I'd always felt like an outsider
in both my own and my mother's country.
A gnat on the window, sticking to the glass
with all its got.

# Wannabe

There's a new… virus?
Pandemic? Epidemic?
I don't even know what to call it.
Maybe it was always there, lurking
in the shadows or maybe it's
resurfaced. And it's only August.

And every time it seems I've got a handle-
got a hold on something, it slips. Dog days
are nearly over and I'm trying to remember
the last time I got grass stains on the knees
of my jeans. I must've been a preteen.
A practically mythological thing.
Today there's no such thing.

Must've been in Türkiye, yes I must've been.
Because nowhere was I ever so free.
It's what drew me in initially, you see.
My mother never let me run amok,
never let me get dirty. And most certainly
didn't let me cross the street alone.
"This is America, Eda. Anything can
happen, don't act like you don't know!"

I used to write poems in one sitting.
Now they come to me in sentences.
I'm always back at square one.
Find myself barely beginning.

I used to devour novels.
Now I'm barely reading.
*Use a bigger word, Alana.*
Now I'm reading **sporadically.**

It's been this way ever since I crossed
the sea to what would've been better shores.
Except I spend more time indoors than I
ever thought I would. And I can't write like
I used to because it all comes out as a question:
How *do* you feel? How do *you* feel?
I don't know or maybe I forgot.

I'm always supposed to be "eating healthy",
whatever that even means. Just last week, thought
to myself, now I know where I went wrong.
I should've been a dancer. Been a good girl.
Did what my mother told me. At least, while
my life was coming undone at the seams,
I could've looked in the mirror and rejoiced
because I had the perfect dancer's body.
I know it's shallow, forgive me.
*All you had to do was dance, Alana.*

I'm just starting to write poems again.
But all I can hear is music without a melody.
Because songs've become my meal ticket.
Though I'm always hungry. Life's always in the way.
Though I'm not as despondent as I used to be.
Peeling my way through shades of grey.

Maybe I'm concussed, because I can *see* my life
going down the drain. Just don't know how it'll all cease.
Just now learning the value of hope. It tastes bitter
as yearning. I don't want to keep living through things
and lying through my teeth about warped rewards reaped.

Everyone around me's "talking American".
Walking, talking, seeming, bargaining.
Everyone I know's gone blonde or got
nicknames no one calls 'em. A relative
I've known my entire life says he wants
to be one: "A Real American." Though he's
had his citizenship longer than I've existed.
Says a piece of paper isn't what being
"A Real American" is. Yet he can barely
speak English. Looks down on others
working paycheck to paycheck.

Now he says, "You're a guest, just visiting."
Implies Mom and I shouldn't come back
to stay with him. "I wanna be A Real American,
with no baggage, no responsibility." He sounds
ridiculous and his idle town is painted red.
I don't have the energy to tell him they'd
never let him in. I don't tell any of them,
I've never felt American, don't think I'll
ever truly feel it as long as I live.

When Mei, Su and Ting-Ting sang that they
wanted to be like other girls, I got it instantly.
Because I'm tired of pretending it's alright-

even *exciting* being anything other than ordinary.
Sometimes I **do** wanna be like other girls.
Just like them. Just like any other American
girl or at least a *bit* like them.

I want to stop hoping and just start showing up.
All for the taking. Want to make my cake and
eat it too. Isn't that what good ol' Americans do?

# metamorphosis

# Say What I Mean

Wonder how much of my writing I threw away
because I thought it wasn't interesting enough.
I wonder how much of myself I throw away everyday,
because I think *I'm* just not interesting enough.

These days, my mother and I keep fighting.
She's confused why I can't be "happy enough"
or at least act it… enough. I don't know how
to say I don't know. Or rather, I've run out
of ways to say words she couldn't stomach
if I said them another way. Say what I mean to say.

# Aimless

Nine years of this listlessness.
Of not seeing the path before me.
Of being pushed and then free-falling.
I haven't been able to get back up, get
the ball rolling. Life just keeps going.
Everything rotating out of frame.
Keep having to turn away. Make room
for new bad habits. I've grown cold and
combative. I feel my heart beating, but
wonder what it'd feel like if it were touched.

I've grown codependent on the internet's fun
cause I've none of my own. I write songs,
I don't know if you've heard- me knocking.
Once wandered around Times Square on a
weekday morning, it was raining and peaceful;
searching for lost things, even felt like I had
a fighting chance. As I passed by, caught no
one's glance. I was entirely coincidental.
I was passerby in the right place at the right time.

I'm beginning to wonder when I'll feel lucky
to feel alive. Lucky to be here *all* the time.
I try to keep grateful and fear in God. I try
to hope in spite of the odds. Cause isn't that
how it goes? Isn't that how *all* the songs go?

Been so long since I wrote a poem.
Thought when the words came they
wouldn't be these. Thought when the
words returned to me, they'd be soaked
in my own happy. I don't know where
I'm going with this. Why all my words
feel so aimless? No longer know what's true.
I wish I had something to do.

# Big Little Kid

Twenty-two, running off fumes.
Mommy means well, just curious
why I can't be good- like I used to be
such a sweet little kid. Wanna watch
my life like a spectator instead of an
active participant. Used to be such a
sweet little kid. Big little kid, tryna
make the most- make the *best* of it.

Big little kid, always wanted to grow up.
Big little kid, think I've had enough-
of never having enough money and always
trying to make ends meet. Always on the
road. Move houses not homes. Family's
photos of people I thought I'd known. It'd just
be nice, something familiar to call my own.
Wanted to leave, now I'm scared to go.

Always trying to be the best. Devoted myself
to others whims, then wonder why I've
developed a savior complex. All my friends
are imaginary. Used to get homesick.
Now I'm too tired to feel any of it.

Used to be such a sweet little kid.
Now I sleepwalk, don't exist. It's me,
I'm always trying to lift: heavy as a

blanket of snow, cold as a corpse.
Trying to lift deadweight, *oh wait-* it's me
rolling over in my own grave. Used to be
such a sweet little kid. Now I talk but
don't speak. Am looked at, not seen.
Rotting and ruining, someone I don't
wanna be. Unable to blossom, deceived
like The Giving Tree. Robbed of my fruit.
What more do you want from me?

Everything was swept out from under me.
Where *do* I get a life? Smothered the desire
to live, cause I had to stay alive. Haven't lived
in a long time. Not happy, just fine.

Mommy says be grateful.
Mommy says it could be worse.
Big girls don't cry.
What if everything hurts?

# Happy

Decade between us in age. She's so vibrant and
full of life, the way I used to be. These days, I've
been questioning what it means to be happy.
Mommy made my favorite foods. We baked
a cake, like a little kid, I licked the spoon.
Reread a chapter out of my favorite book.
Frequented the cinema just last week.

*Happiness, is that you?*

Haven't dressed up in a long time
Had a moment alone- had a good time.
Had something truly *all* mine.

Says she wants to grow up and be a woman.
I think that's where everything good ended.
Did I want too much or just fall too far?
Not just any other woman is born a star.

She's still so happy. Lives life like it's a party.
She *is* the life of the party. I feel her gaze
in the mirror, how she admires me. Aspires
to me. Someone who's not had a brush with
happy in so long it scares me.

No one told me where to mine dopamine?
Why is it never after me- chasing me? Like I

chase childhood. Chase the fantasy. A kind
of happy you don't pay to be. But now isn't life-
isn't our every waking move made of money?
Maybe it's why I'm broke, never have enough
to pay with, you see.

Says she wants to grow up and be a woman.
I know that it's the truth.

"When I grow up, I want to be just like you."

# Music Man

Music man in the dank Woodhaven underpass.
Brow knit tight. for as long as I reach back for
the memory. He is mandatory. A devout constant
in a transient existence. Music playing on. in the
ballroom of my mind. He grows old and weary,
doubt he'd remember me. Seems he hasn't looked
up from the Erhu in a decade. Incline my head just
so, in acknowledgment. Though he remains oblivious,
I will mourn a tomorrow without music- without him in it.

I never caught his name and it's the funniest thing.
If you asked me how his melody goes. I couldn't tell you.

# Paradoxes

There is a dog with no leash, no companion
or master. Fur a wealthy black and brown.
He lounges in the sand, carries himself so like
a pharaoh. By God, does he appear regal.
Though he belongs to the streets, lives among
soot coated beasts, baying. Bounding off in
hot pursuit of their next prey. Rip newborn
kittens' hearts clean of their bodies. Leave guts
bedraggled- splayed across the pavement.
Bloodbath outside my window. No time for
funerals, off they go after the elderly and the
disabled. After children who've just taken
the training wheels off their bicycles.

The pharaoh never entertained the chase until
winter came and hunger begged. Then the
pharaoh toppled. Became just as ordinary.
Just as unrestrained.

I was eighteen, still learning people can be
two things at once: wild and elegant.
I was nineteen, when I understood it.

Watched *The Last Black Man in San Francisco.*
Montgomery illustrates cruel men with humility.
Depicts them with such reverence. Says,
"I shouldn't get to appreciate them because
they're mean to me? That's silly."


Could never justify why I loved the first
person I ever did. Was simply at peace with it.
Knew only in time could I put the feelings
to bed. At first they were so mean. Thought,
*what does this say about me?* Winters became
springs. I learned they were beautiful as they
were inexplicable. Fat-hearted and cruel.
Too good for their own good, but loved
to toy with people's emotions, too.

Knew I needed to grow a backbone way
back in middle school. Grew a bitch in a
terrarium to survive. She's as malicious
as I am kind. Naive and barbaric.
Wild and elegant. Fat-hearted and cruel.

Paradoxes are me and you.

# Home

I'm still waiting to come home.
Though I'm not sure where home is yet.

The dogs I've wanted since I was a child
are scratching at the door, waiting to play.
The friends I wished on stars for, are in
my kitchen, baking. My mother tends to
her garden. I make sure she finally has
her Eden. And we don't have to run
anymore. When we do, we run along home.

And maybe- just *maybe,* there's someone
to care for me. Lingering on my skin like
body mist. Waiting to let me in. The sun
is setting and I'm trying, believe me,
I'm trying to come home.

# About the Author

Alana Eda Johnson is a 23 year old native New Yorker. After spending many summers in her beloved Türkiye, Alana decided to split her time between two concrete jungles: Istanbul and New York City. Alana's youth was spent writing way too many songs, short stories and diary entries. Her love for poetry blossomed in elementary school, after an assignment prompted her to wax poetic about the fulfillment only an apple (her favorite fruit at the time) could bring. *Secrets That Speak* is a passion project composed of the experiences, feelings and circumstances of youth, girlhood, adult and womanhood. This book was sewn together out of the poems scribbled on stray homework assignments and dog-eared senior thesis drafts. This book was a dream; Alana's mother, as always, turned another one of her daughter's dreams into a reality.

# Acknowledgments

There is only one person I'd like all of us to thank and that is my mother, for pushing me to do more and do better. Pushing me to be bolder, be more out there, be more confident and fearless. Without my mother, this book would not be in any of our hands.

X: @alanaedajohnson

Instagram: @thealanaedajohnson

YouTube: Alana Eda Johnson

Email: alanajohnson2001@gmail.com